ELEPHANT COLORING BOOK FOR ADULTS

Realistic Coloring Books For Adults, Advanced Elephant Coloring Book For Stress Relief and Relaxation

Realistic Animals Coloring Book: Vol 12

by Amanda Davenport

ISBN-13: 978-1533537430

ISBN-10: 1533537437

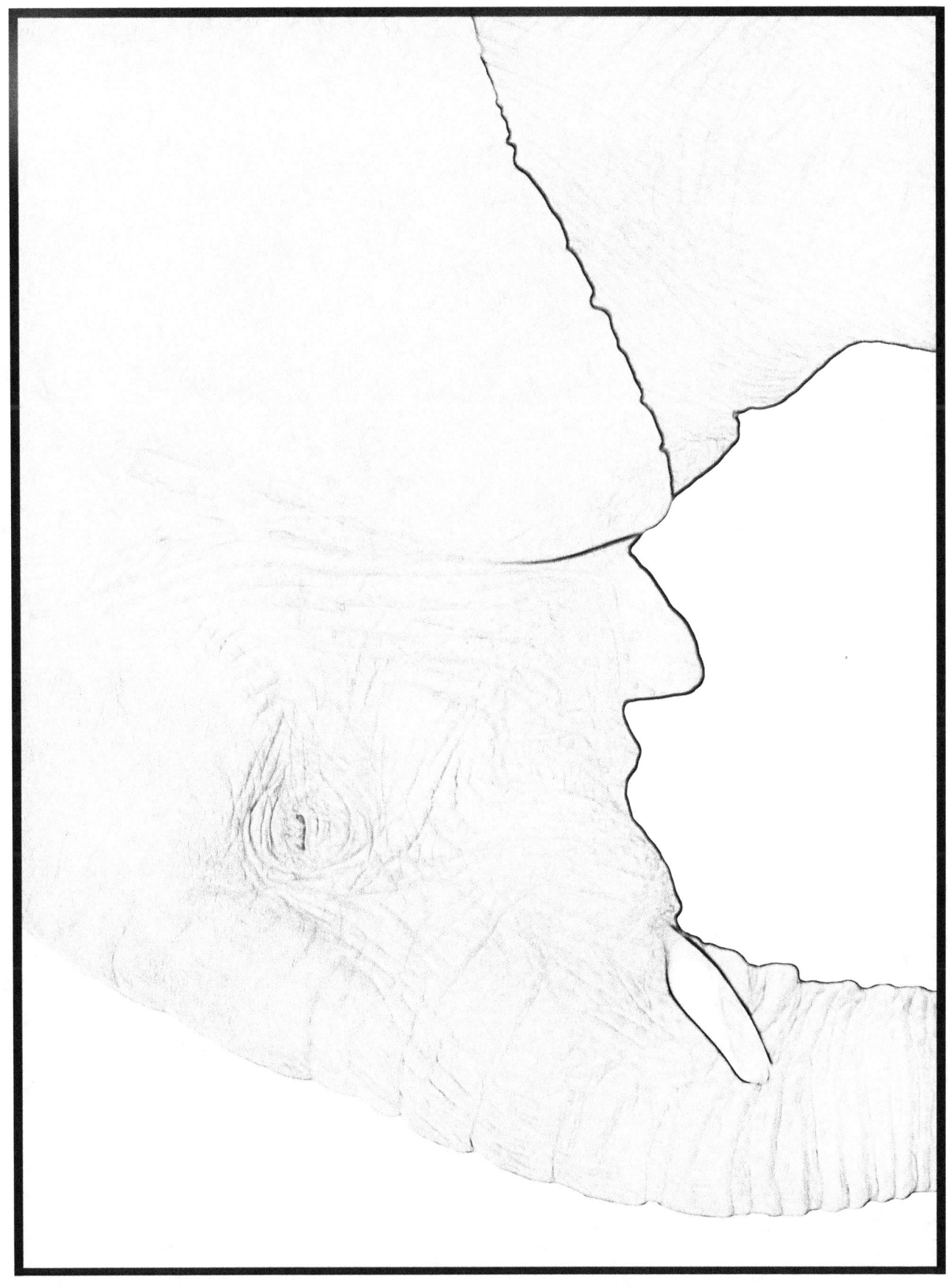

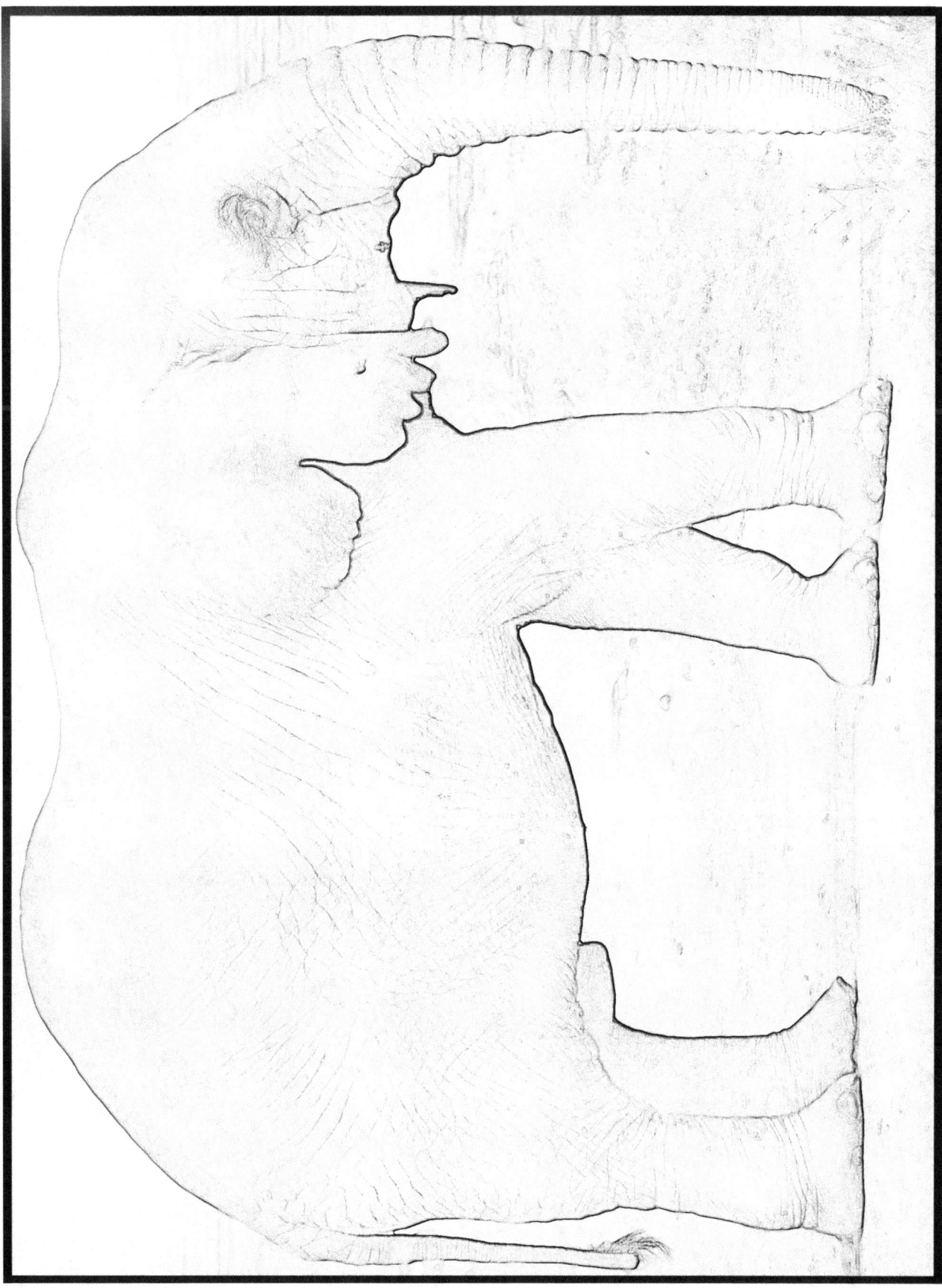

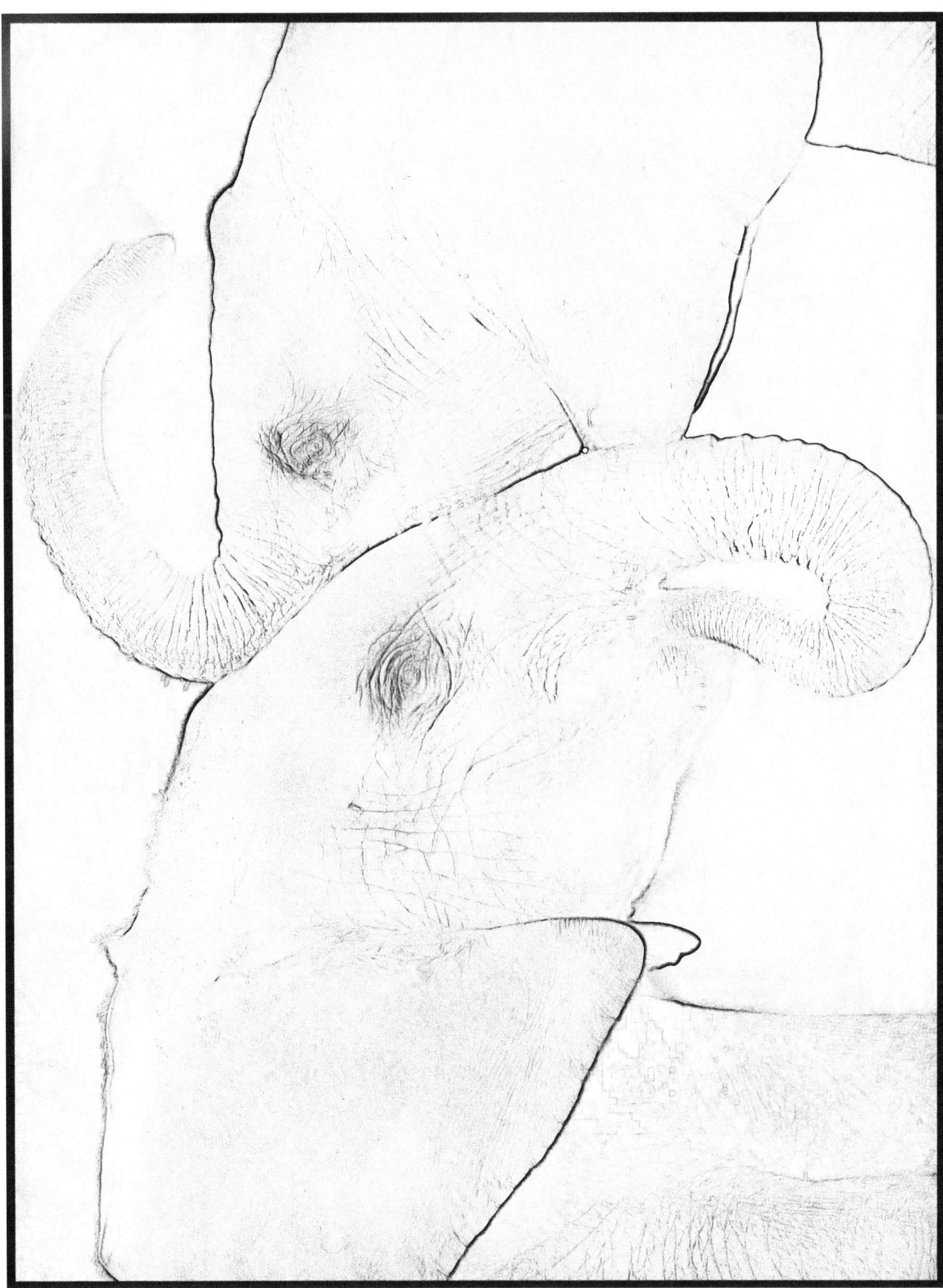

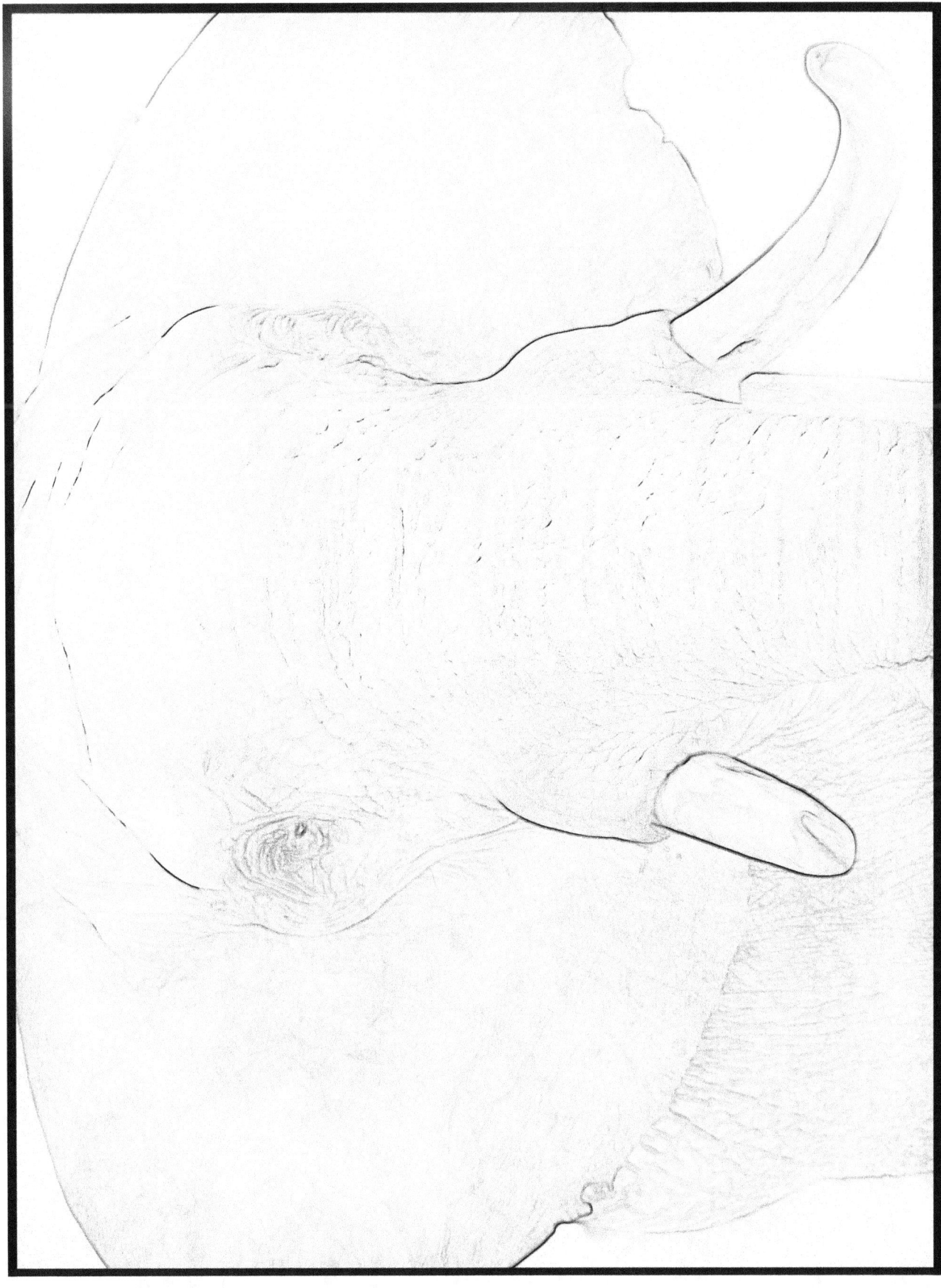

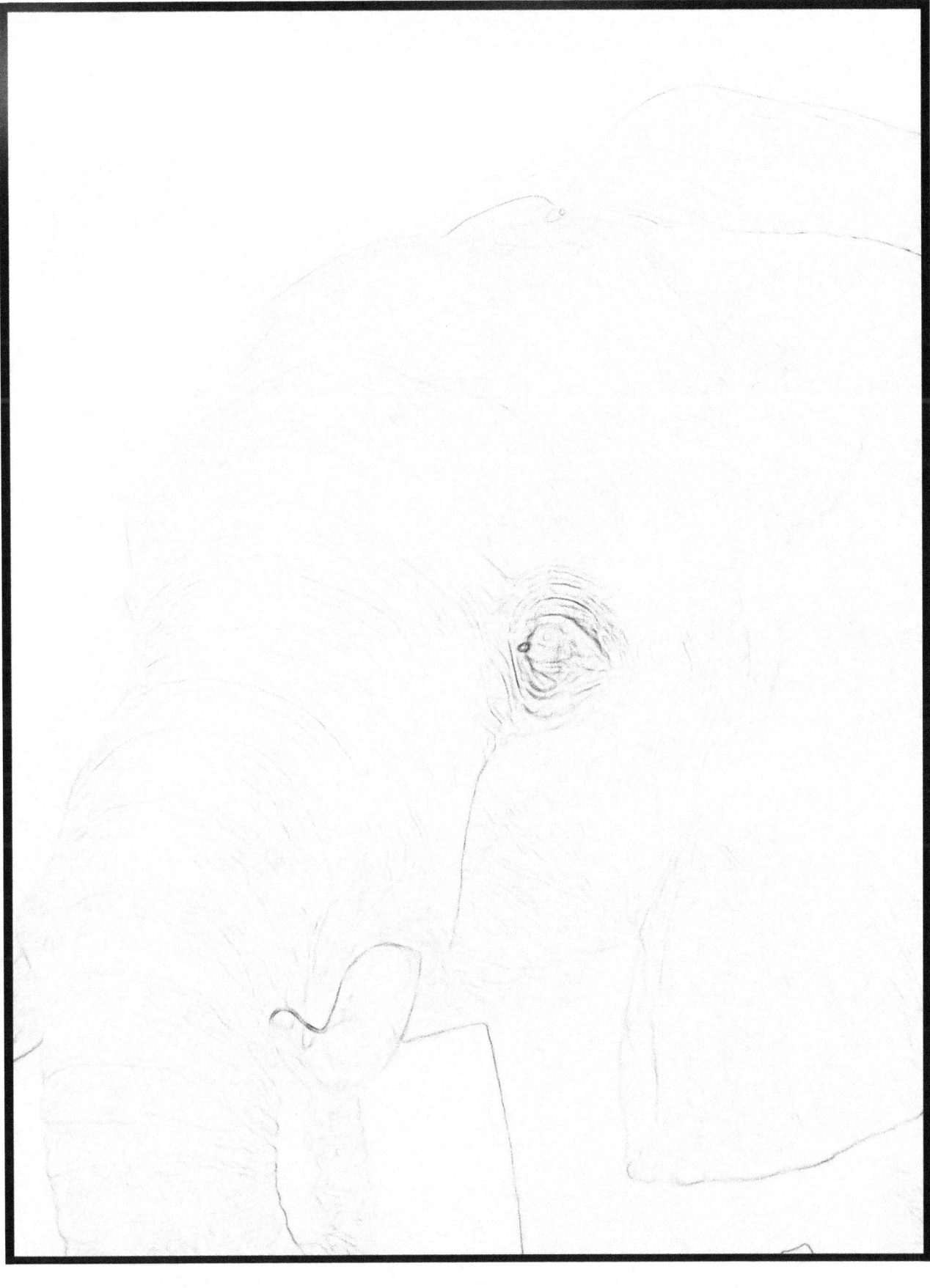

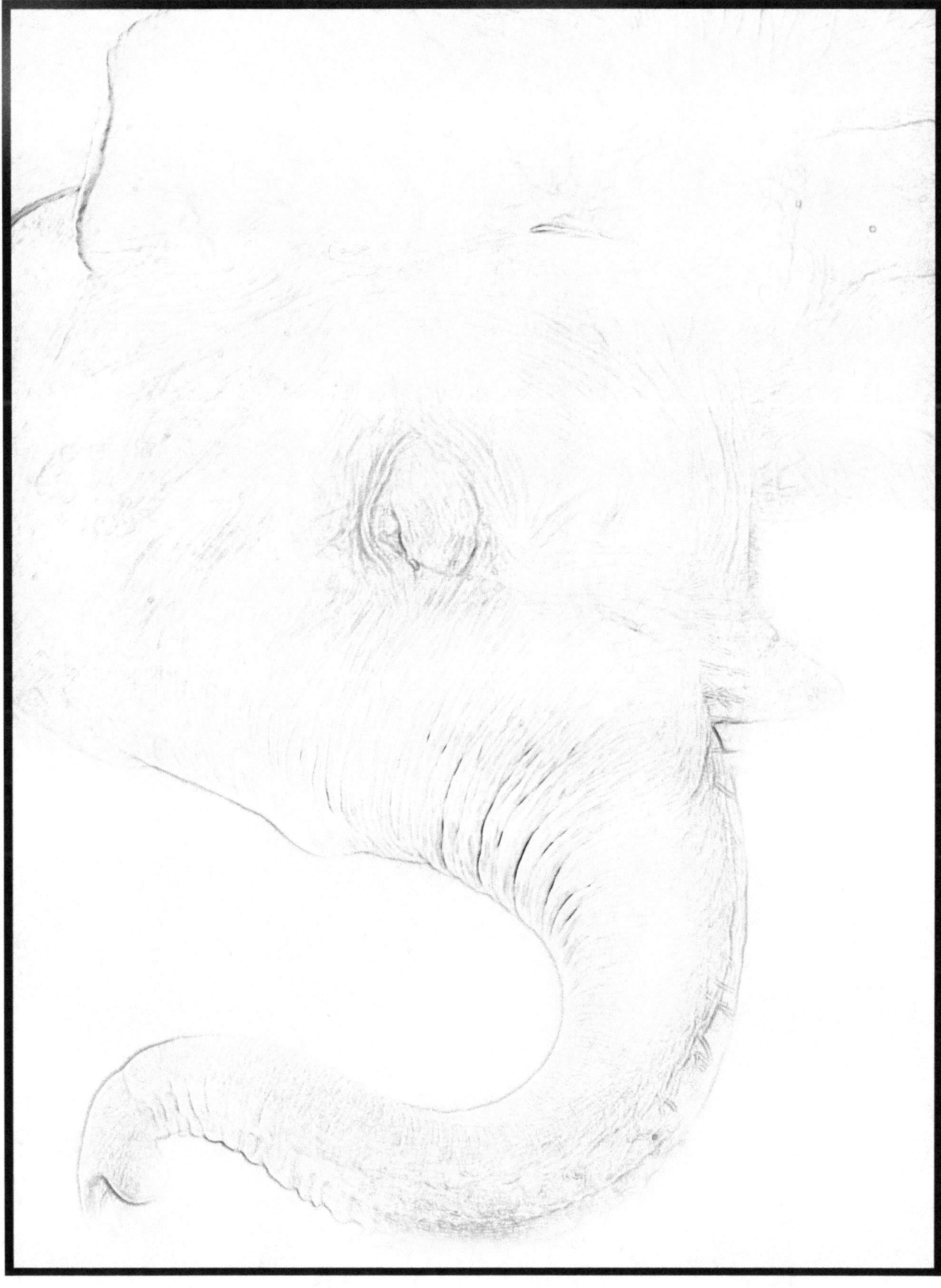

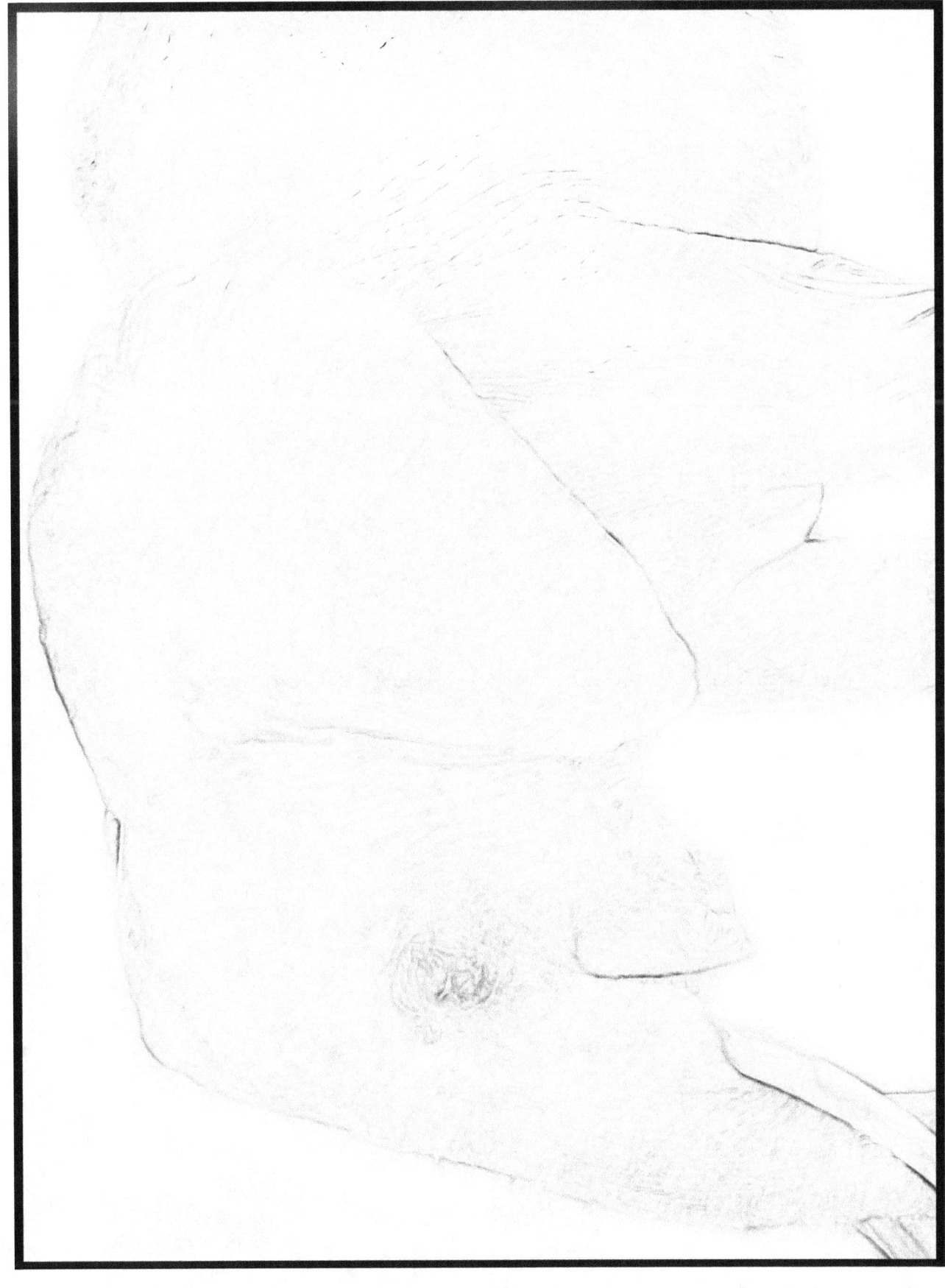

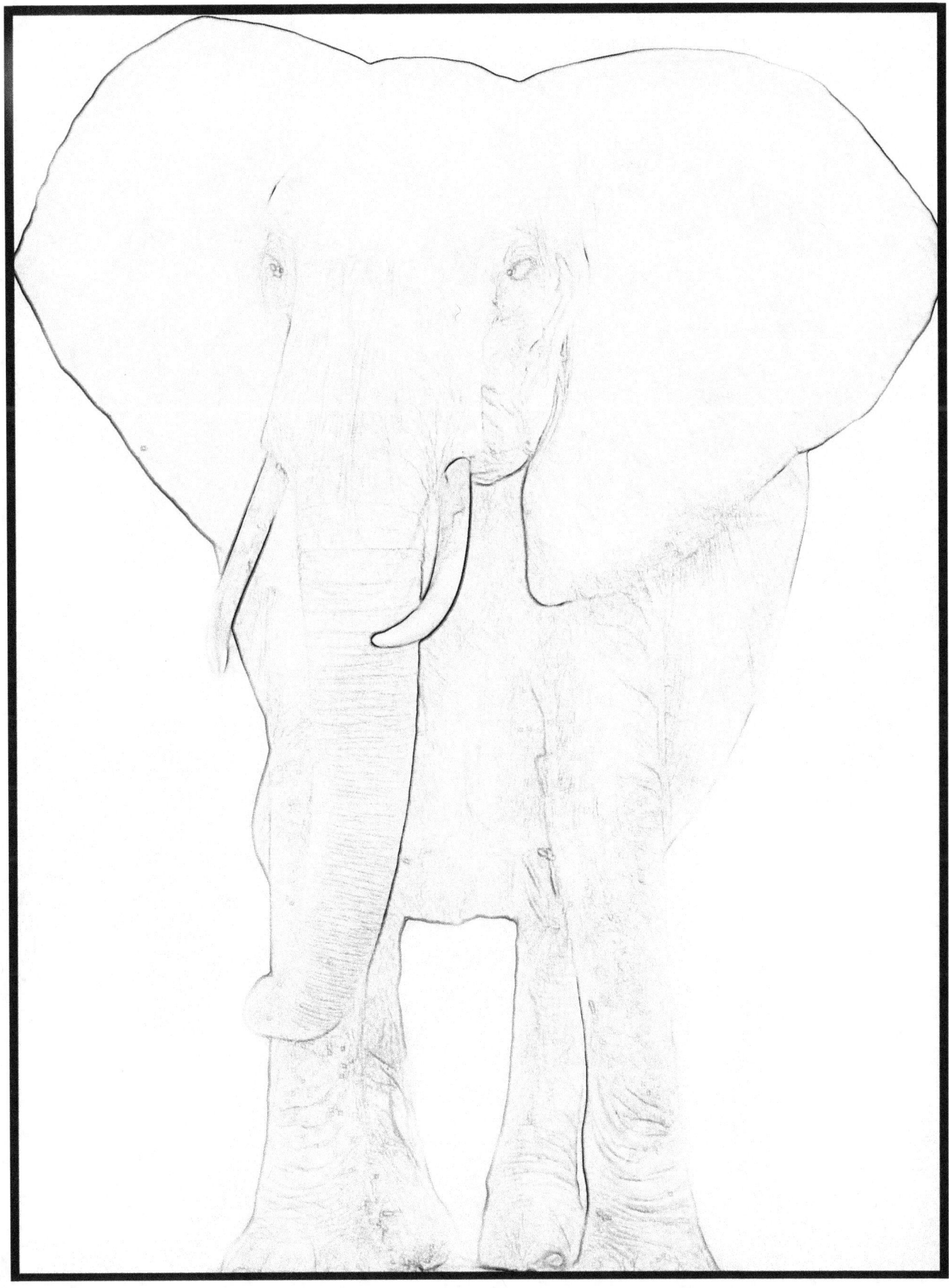

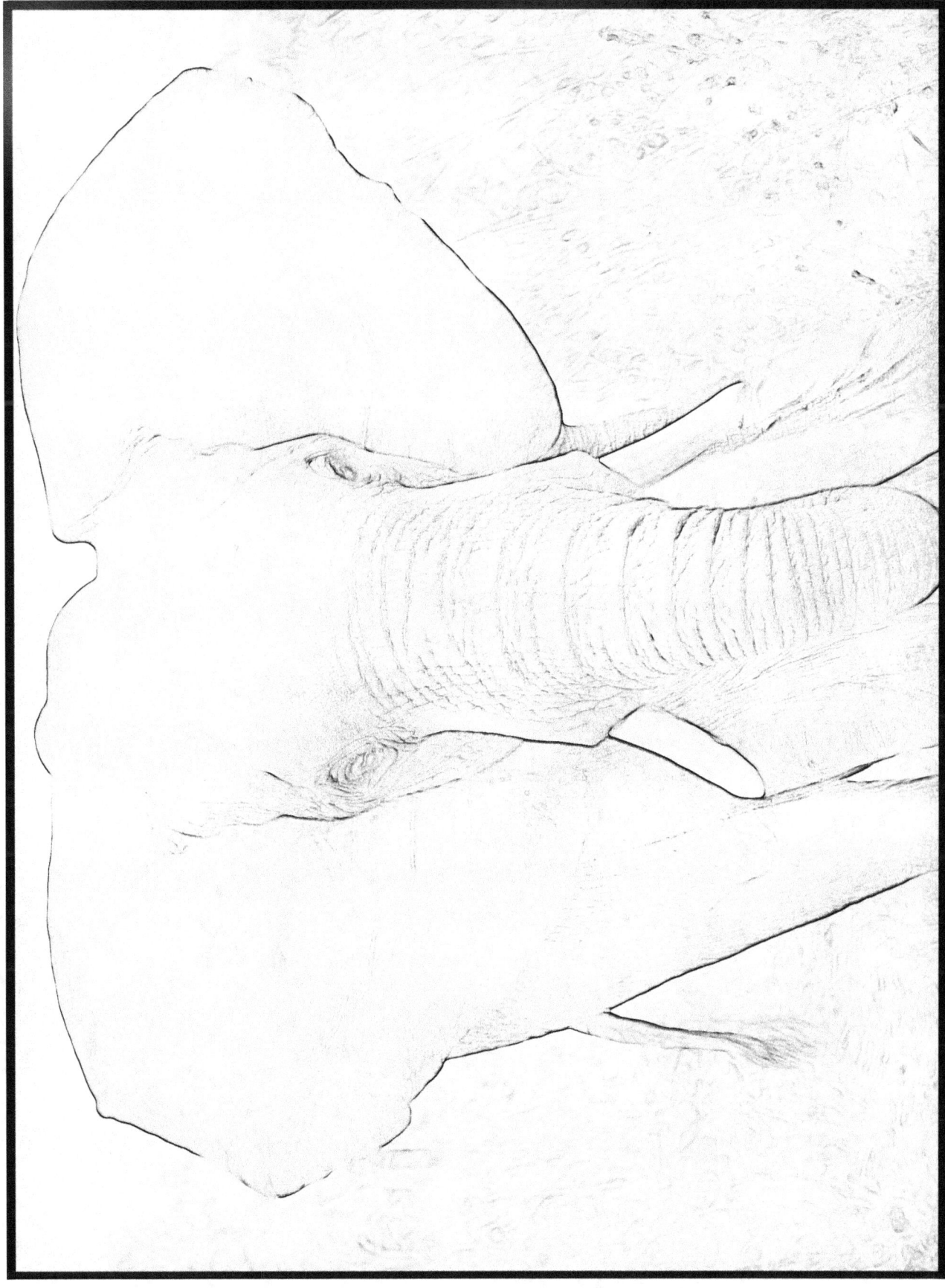

COLOR TEST PAGE

COLOR TEST PAGE